A VERY SPECIAL GOD TOUCHES A VERY ORDINARY GUY

Howard S. Gifford

ACKNOWLEDGMLENTS

I wish to extend my appreciation to my wife, Sandra, for her editing, typing and overall advice in preparing this book. I also wish to thank Sandra for her love and support throughout the many years of our marriage.

Chapter I

It was a hot summer Saturday on August 17, 1929 when I made my entrance into the world and was given the name of Howard Samuel Gifford. My parents were Samuel and Dorothy Gifford.

It is interesting how my family all came together. My paternal grandparents were Samuel and Margaret Gifford. Samuel was born 1874 in Port Republic, NJ, and lived in Atlantic City, NJ. Margaret, born in 1867, came over from Dungannon, County Tyrone, in Northern Ireland in 1888. She worked in Haddonfield, NJ as a domestic. The circumstances as to how she got to Atlantic City and met Samuel is unknown. Later they were married at a mass wedding ceremony by the Salvation Army in Atlantic City in 1895. Margaret and Samuel both had been singing on the boardwalk, she with a tambourine.

My Grandfather, Samuel T. Gifford , was a conductor for the Pennsylvania-Reading Seashore Line traveling from Camden to Atlantic City. Samuel and his wife, Margaret, wanted to start a family, but unfortunately she had six pregnancies which all died either in childbirth or a few days later. But they did not give up. She became pregnant a seventh time, this time with my father. Life was not easy by any means. At the delivery the doctor looked at Samuel and said, "We may lose this baby, your wife, or both of them." This was a great shock. You can imagine the heartbreak Samuel and the family felt. There had been many prayers for both Margaret and the baby. She had overheard the conversation between Samuel and the doctor. Knowing Christ as her personal Savior and that dying in this life and going to heaven to meet her Savior would be fine, she whispered to her husband, "If one of has to go, then I hope it is me, and the lad will live and be a man of God.' (Later I found out from her sister that she meant a preacher of the Gospel). My grandmother did go home to be with the Lord, and the baby, named Samuel, lived to become my Dad. Samuel, my grandfather, was now in a difficult situation – left with a new-born baby. He soon married another Christian woman, Eva Hubbs. They had one boy, Milton, and four girls, Alice, Thelma, Ruth and Jenny. I grew up knowing Eva as my grandmother.

On my maternal side Howard Lupton, my grandfather, whom I was named after, went to Camden from Bridgeton (reason unknown) and met and married Bertha Storm. They had one daughter, Dorothy, and one son, Charles. .Dorothy was born in Camden, NJ in 1906. We believe Dorothy and Samuel met at Parkside Methodist Church in Camden, NJ.

In the year before I was born and the year after, tragedy struck in two heart wrenching ways. My mother's brother, Charles, at the age of eleven, was hit and killed by a bus on Haddon Avenue in the Parkside section of Camden. My mother, Dorothy, was deeply saddened and so moved by the loss of her brother that she and my father delayed their wedding until 1928. The other tragedy affected my grandfather, Howard R. Lupton, who was in real estate in 1929, in Camden and due to the depression lost the properties he owned, including ten houses which he had under construction, and even the very home in which he and his family resided. Eventually Howard and Bertha moved in with my parents and me, along with Bertha's mother, Cecelia Brewin Storm.

My parents had rented a small apartment on the 800 block of

Haddon Avenue in Collingswood. Now with a new baby and three more adults moving in my parents needed more room. They all moved to a larger home on the corner of Haddon and Madison in Collingswood. I have no idea how my father handled all this because he had not graduated from high school and did not have a trade. He was always a hard worker. He worked as a parking lot attendant and later at the shipyard and never complained. They tell me I pushed my stroller down the whole flight of stairs - from the second to the first floor. Though I cried a bit I sustained no serious injury. Some might question this, however.

I really had a great dad. He worked long hours to support his family and we had many great times when we got together. He never had a piano lesson in his life but he could play most anything by ear. After supper many nights we gathered around the piano and sang hymns and also some popular songs. It did not help my singing voice, but it was something I will never forget. Dad usually worked six days a week, but when he was home on Sunday he made pancakes and that was a big deal for me. He had his own parking lot in Philly, before the war and when a gas shortage came it finished his business. He then joined 32,000 others in building aircraft carriers at the New York Ship Building Company in Camden. They worked round the clock, seven days a week. The navy needed those carriers and my dad helped build them.

Then there was always the Christmas Surprise. I was not allowed in the basement after Nov.15th. We had what we called the train platform. During those days leading up to Christmas dad would add some new aspects to "the platform." I had two trains. One was a typical Lionel train with engine, coal car, and passenger cars. I took good care of it and it still runs. Also I had a light weight American Flier. I would put it at one end of the track, turn it on full power and watch it fly off the other end. This was frowned on by the parents, but lots of fun!

Speaking of family, five years after I was born, a little sister, Margaret (Peggy) was added to our family. Peggy and I had many good times together, growing up. We all thought out family was complete, but when I was seventeen years old we found out that my mother was going to have another baby. We were all thrilled when on July 7. 1945 Nancy Lee arrived. Lots of things changed with a new baby. The two girls had many good times to share. Unfortunately as I was older, I was soon away from home.

Chapter II

As I said before I had a very happy childhood. I grew up in the very "teeth" of the depression. but I did not realize it. I was poor and did not know it. I always had food to eat and clothes to wear. Sometimes we had a car and sometimes we did not. I began my public school education at Tatum School in Collingswood in 1934. I was a good student and was well received by my progression of teachers. I had learned discipline from my parents and was not a problem in school. In sixth grade I was chosen with five others to receive the "Tri-School Dad's Merit Award" which was chosen for doing good work scholastically and general good behavior.

For seventh grade I went to the Junior High School and continued to be a good student, getting mostly A's and B's but my real interest was in sports. Collingswood was well known as a football powerhouse under the leadership of Coach Skeetz Irvine for over thirty years. My grandfather introduced me to Ted Laux and Willard Bisbing about 1936 and I set my heart to be as good as they were and excel in football for Collingswood. I was on the football team in ninth and tenth grades and was in the starting backfield. At the end of the tenth grade season I contracted whooping cough and it left me with a slight heart murmur. The doctor said no more football and that really broke my heart. In my senior year I went out for baseball as a catcher and coach Bill Diemer kindly gave me a suit and I was able to earn a letter, mostly sitting on the bench.

As I continued through grades ten to twelve I developed an increasing interest in aircraft and decided to study to be an aeronautical engineer. Drexel Institute of Technology was a very well-known school located right in Philadelphia. I applied for admission and took a competitive test and was accepted. Since money was a factor I also took a competitive test for a two year scholarship. I took the test and was thrilled to receive a scholarship. I attended Drexel from September 1947 until June of 1949. during which time I spent two six month periods working at Glenn Martin Aircraft outside of Baltimore, MD. Drexel was very hard academically but I was receiving passing grades until the January to June session. In January 1949 something happened that changed my life completely.

One of my first recollections is going to church. We attended the First Methodist Church at Park and Dayton Avenues. The sanctuary was a large grey stone building with a large Sunday School on the other end. I remember when we had a terrible fire in 1932 and it was mostly demolished. We had to go to Sunday School in Van Meter's Garage near the railroad. Sunday School was held at 2:30 P.M. in those days and our family went every Sunday. More important than the building was the solid group of people who believed in Jesus Christ as their personal Savior, and that the Bible was God's inspired Word

Somehow I heard. that teaching, but avoided it until I was nineteen years old. I remember Mr. Alan Campbell taught my Sunday School class at about tenth grade. He was a real Christian engineer so tried to present the gospel in a way we boys would understand its importance and receive Christ as Savior, but we were a bunch of typical guys and interested in other things. I agreed with what he said but it did not have relevance in my life. My interests were sports, girls and school in that order.

During this time I freely went to worship and Sunday School, but I did not want to go to Youth Group. (then called MYF). My mom insisted I go and I insisted I not go. We went round and round each Sunday evening. The friends I had were mostly into sports and the young people at church were not. Finally mom won out, and I went unwillingly (as John Wesley did to Aldersgate) . I attended the meetings and met some new friends but nothing much changed in my life.

Our church was very evangelistic. Each year we would bring in a traveling evangelist and have a week of evangelistic services with moving music and Bible preaching plus an invitation to come forward to the altar to receive Jesus as one's personal Savior. I was aware of this but didn't usually attend. Our pastor, Rev. Harry F. Henry, became inspired and declared that he would be the evangelist. He called the special meetings "The Fellowship of Redemption." They were well attended and many surrendered their lives to Christ.

Friday night was "Youth night" and all the youth were urged to attend. I had not been attending the MYF meetings very long, but somehow was elected President. As it was youth night I was expected to go to the pulpit and lead in prayer. I did this without much anxiety. The service proceeded and then came the sermon. Dr. Henry was not preaching that night as they had brought in a younger preacher to reach the youth. I have no idea what he said, BUT when he invited people to come to the altar and receive Jesus Christ as their Savior something happened to me that had never happened before. I was terribly uncomfortable. I felt very wrong and knew I should go to the altar. But I was a very shy person and said to myself, "there's no way I'm going up there." Then he said, "If you are hesitant to come up, ask the person next to you to go with you" That was just right for me. I asked Tom Naglee, sitting next to me, to go with me. I knelt at the altar and prayed. Several adults explained what I needed to do to respond to whoever was making me so miserable. (I learned later "He" was the Holy Spirit) and gave myself to Jesus Christ to be my Savior. Everybody around me was very happy and was praising God. This was all very new to me and I wasn't so sure my life would be different as they were telling me, but I was very sure I had responded to Whoever was speaking to me in my heart. There was no radical change the next day, but many things did begin to change in my life. I had a lot to learn and a long way to go, but what happened that night changed everything.

I continued to live at home, commuting to Drexel. This experience of meeting Christ at the altar happened in January and I was in school until June. From June to December I was on a six month period in industry, which for me was Glenn Martin Aircraft in Middle River, MD. At this time I realized that my life had really changed and I no longer wanted to be an aeronautical engineer and make a lot of money. One Sunday evening Vincent Joy, a young man from our local church, and his wife, Becky, who had started a mission in Copper Center , AK were home and he sang a song that deeply stirred my heart

Oh how well do I remember how I doubted day by day,
For I did not know for certain that my sins were washed away
When the Spirit tried to tell me,, I would not truth receive
I endeavored to be happy and make myself believe.
But it's real, It's real, O I know it's real.
Praise God the doubts are settled and I know,
I know it's real.

That song touched the bottom of my heart. I, too, knew it was real. And my sins were forgiven. I was thrilled with knowing Jesus Christ and I wanted to spend all my life telling others. JESUS IS REAL! I believe that was the beginning of my call to the ministry of the Gospel.

Several things changed at that point. I was no longer enrolled at

Drexel so I came home from working at Glenn Martin in Middle River. I wanted to go to Asbury College to study for the ministry. I had no money, so I went to work at the local A&P Supermarket. I was able to take twelve hours at Temple University Theological Seminary during this time, along with John Ewing, a young pastor who was driving to school. I worked at the A & P until September and then went to Asbury College, which is now Asbury University. I had been dating a fine Christian girl and we saw a lot of each other at various church activities so when I went to Asbury there were a lot of letters back and forth and happy visits at home.

I knew I had an inner experience of Jesus Christ as my Savior and was living in the great joy of my many young Christian friends at First Church. All the while I was seeking a deeper experience with Christ, called sanctification. I hoped it would happen at Asbury. Although I had many good times and met some really deep Christians I was not satisfied with my own inner life. I went to the altar after many services seeking this deeper life or sanctification. It didn't happen. I wanted a deep emotional experience and could not get it. All the time this girl and I were writing back and forth and getting closer in our relationship. I became depressed at it all. I began to doubt our relationship. But God's hand was always on me and there were many evidences of His presence. Money was always a big issue. By the middle of November my meal ticket had run out. There were days when I did not eat. As Thanksgiving day neared I wondered about my Thanksgiving meal at Asbury. I heard the meal was ninety cents. (A very different economy than now.) On Wednesday I received a card in the mail from my Aunt Velma back in Collingswood. In the card was a one dollar bill. Ninety cents for my Thanksgiving dinner and ten cents for tithe. Is God faithful? That was a sure assurance to me of His faithfulness. I came home for Christmas Holiday and then faced going back to Asbury and tuition. As usual I had no money. I knew God had called me to preach but I had no money for tuition. Sometime between Christmas and New Year's Day this fine Christian girl and I went alone to the sanctuary of our church. We knelt at the altar in the dark and prayed "what do I do? Go back to Asbury with no money or stay home and forget the ministry." We were both assured that I should go back to

12

Asbury. God did provide! Any thinking person would say I must have lost my mind. But the fact was I now had a new mind in Christ! The just shall live by faith!

Chapter III

I went back to Asbury with no money. When it became time to register I was praying. I began to get mail from Collingswood. Some had ten dollars and some had twenty, and so on. I forget all the figures, but somehow people from my home church knew my need and were sending the money. I had enough to pay my bill. PRAISE GOD! HE IS ABLE. I had enough money to pay for that quarter and the next. I even had enough to pay $13.00 to the hospital in Lexington when I split my thumb playing basketball.

But in spite of all this I was still seeking this deeper spiritual life. I read several books written by people who had this experience and I wanted it. I felt I could not be the pastor God wanted me to be without this spiritual power. I put everything on the altar for Jesus. This wasn't very much as I had no money, no house, no car, but everything was His. There was still one problem! This fine Christian girl I was dating and planning to marry. Time after time, when I was in a service where the Holy Spirit was moving, He said to me "No" to marrying this girl. She was a fine Christian and would be a great help in the ministry. I could not understand in my mortal mind. Again and again it was "no". Finally I said "yes" and prayerfully talked with her and we ended our relationship. I felt terrible. I was confused. But I did it. This still did not give me the spiritual experience I wanted and I began to be depressed.

I stayed at home for a year and worked at the A & P as I had previously. I saved all I could, but hesitated to go back to Asbury. Then someone suggested Houghton College, which was a Wesleyan College with the same beliefs as Asbury. I had been praying with

Olive Gilbert about what I should do. College had started for the fall semester. Olive knew a professor at Houghton named Dr. George Failing. She called him and I could be admitted about two weeks after the semester began. I took an all-day train out of North Philadelphia station. I arrived in Olean, NY about 6:00 PM. David Naglee, a Houghton student, and my best friend from back home, picked me up in his car in Olean and took me back about 8:00 PM. The whole student body and administration was at near-by Letchworth Park at a picnic. One administrator had agreed to stay at the college so I could enroll by 8:30 PM. So, by the skin of my teeth I became a student of the college as a Junior.

My first class was an American History Class on the third floor of Luckey Building. (I will come back to this later as it was a big factor in my life.) I was assigned a class schedule and a roommate. So here I am, a student at Houghton College studying for the ministry of the Gospel. I met some people, attended classes and went to some social events. I attended the Wesleyan Methodist Church in Houghton where Rev. Edward Angell was the pastor. He was a very good preacher of the Gospel and all the students loved him.

What a thrill it was to be at Houghton in 1951 when revival broke out on the campus. After two weeks of evangelistic services, when some lives were touched, it was on several people's hearts that there were a lot of spiritual needs that were still unmet. Doc Jo was a leader of a small group who were in prayer about these needs. After the final Sunday night service, Doc Jo and some others were at the altar of the church praying for a real revival. One by one young people began to arrive at the church. God began to meet their needs and they returned to the dorms for more students until the church was full. Many of the girls were in bathrobes when they arrived. The marvelous thing about it was that this was a real Holy Ghost revival and with no human in charge. Rev. Angel and President Paine were seated in the front row of the church and no one was on the platform leading the service. The entire group was singing the praises of God. A person would sense their need to get right with God, go to the altar and pray, stand and give their testimony of what happened in their heart and return to their seat. This happened again and again. This continued throughout most of the night.

The next day each class would be broken up with testimonies and praise to God for spiritual victory. This happened throughout most of the week. Students went out from the campus to the surrounding area to churches and other colleges to share their testimony of what God was doing in their lives. Remember this was a Christian College and most of the students came there with a Christian experience, but some had drifted spiritually and some were questioning their call to Christian service. Things like that were getting straightened out by the Holy Spirit and the whole campus was aflame with God's power. My own heart was stirred and I will never forget that night when God Himself was in charge.

Arriving late as I did, I did not get to play football that season, but I did get to play baseball, and both sports again in my senior year. A very big factor was that I was able to change my room assignment. I moved into Barnett Cottage, a summer cottage on the camp meeting grounds, adjacent to the campus. Dave Naglee and eight other Christian guys lived there who were eventually to become a medical doctor, a teacher and three ministers. We didn't do anything wrong, but we had a lot of fun, and living in that fellowship was a big factor in defeating my depression.

The biggest factor in meeting my desire for the Sanctification experience was the life and teaching of Dr. Claude Ries. He was an ordained Wesleyan Methodist preacher who had been teaching at Houghton for some time. Since I had taken Beginning Greek at Asbury and spiritually blessed by it, I decided to take two years of Greek with Dr. Ries, which amounted to a Greek Minor. This was a true man of God. One evening he invited me up to his home and we talked a lot about Wesleyan Sanctification. He called it "the deeper life" and had written his doctorate on that subject. He gave me a signed copy of his doctorate and to this day I refer to it often. I also took a minor in Psychology which would be helpful in counselling in the ministry. I also took several Bible courses from Dr. Bert Hall who was a younger man and also very spiritual. One other thing happened in these classes. I met a young lady, named Sandra Fisher. She was also a Bible major and Psych Minor so we had many classes together.

16

Chapter IV

Sandra and I became good friends over the next two years. I dated a couple girls during this time but nothing serious. Then two things happened about the same time. I liked Sandy a lot and decided to ask her to the Varsity Banquet in April of my senior year. Sadie Hawkins Day came shortly before this. For this day the girls chased the boys. Everything was turned around. The girls carried the boys books, held the doors open for them, etc. Sandy caught me for this affair and I was real glad. This event and the Varsity Banquet during the final weeks of school were special times, plus we had many other good times together. My folks came up for graduation and they, Sandy and I did some things together. Graduation was over and it was time to go home. Sandy had come up to the cottage to say goodbye. As we were still just good friends at this time there was no big kiss as I had vowed not to get involved with any girls and then hurt them. But as the car pulled away and I looked back at Sandy I could see tears running down her cheeks. Wow! There must be more going on here than I realized.

I arrived home and was confused as what to do. I felt inadequate in going on in the ministry, yet I felt that was God's call. Sandy had another year of college and we wrote back and forth. I knew that I had been deferred from the military draft because I was in college, so I decided to volunteer for the draft to get things moving and was inducted into the US Army in September, 1953. I didn't mind being in the Army and the Lord opened many doors for me. Sandy and I continued to write more and more. When she graduated from Houghton in June of 1954, she accepted a position at Quincy EUB Orphanage in

Father, Sam Gifford

Mother and I

Mother, Dorothy Gifford

1933 with Dad

1937

Always Loved football!

Ocean City 19

Big glasses in the '70"S!

80th Birthday

College Graduation — 1953

Wedding Bells, Erie, PA , 1956

Our children, Christmas 2015

Ireland 2009 with cousins

Family Reunion at America's Keswick, 2015

Pennsylvania. Meanwhile I had been assigned to a Signal Battalion at Fort Meade, MD which was just outside of Baltimore. It was about 100 miles from there to Quincy. Before long I was making more and more trips to visit Sandy and we realized we were deeply in love and looked forward to those occasional weekends. A couple on the staff at Quincy had a home there and designated one room as Howard's room. I would wear my uniform up there so I could easily hitchhike. Then I would change into my civvies while I was there, often with a three-day pass. I was still in my "spiritual funk" and did not want to make a commitment until I was sure about the ministry. One weekend I had a three-day pass, took the train from Baltimore to Philadelphia, got my dad's car, drove back to Quincy and picked up Sandy. Then we drove back to Collingswood, NJ and spent Saturday and Sunday at my folks home. I drove Sandy back to Quincy Sunday night and later drove back to Fort Meade. I got into Fort Meade about two or three AM. I had to get up early and stand revelry, but I knew it was pay day and I would get off at noon. I then proceeded to drive my dad's car back to Collingswood. I remember crossing the Delaware Memorial Bridge around 3:00 PM, but the next thing I knew I had fallen asleep, just missing a concrete overpass. That would have been the end of my life right there, but even though the car rolled over onto its top, I did not receive any injuries at all. THANK YOU, JESUS! The State Police came and were very kind as I was in uniform, but still had to give me a ticket for falling asleep. The car was damaged on the roof, and the windshield was damaged. The trooper said I could drive the car if it was safe. I realized it was safe and drove home, although I did not go back on the Turnpike! Here I had totaled my dad's car, but he was very kind. The very first thing he said after I told him of the accident was to ask if supper was ready. So we ate supper and then looked at the car. His only comment was "you did have a little accident, didn't you?" Those were the good old days when insurance was insurance. We drove out to Rohrer's Chevrolet, got another 1950 Chevy, and I think I paid $50.00.

I was discharged from the Army in September, 1955 and went to work at the Camden Rescue Mission. Now we are separated. I am in Collingswood and Sandy is in Quincy. Again, many letters! Sandy came to my home for Christmas, expecting an engagement ring and received a pair of bedroom slippers. What a disappointment! I was such a nut. I drove a big truck for the Mission and collected old furniture and newspapers so the Mission could minister to men who lived on the street. They were drunks and homeless. We fed them an evening meal, gave them a Gospel Message and a place to sleep. Sandy

and I were still writing and visiting when we were able. One January morning as I read my Bible I was led to Revelation chapter 1 and it clearly pointed to our Lord Jesus Christ. Jesus's message was clear "get moving in the ministry, get enrolled in seminary and marry Sandy." I had the definite assurance that if I did not move now I would lose out. I knew the Gospel was real and I did not want to lose out. I called Sandy that evening, January 13, and asked her to marry me in Erie on February 25. That was very unkind to put that pressure on her and her family, but she agreed. Her mom made her wedding dress for $16.00. We had seventy dollars between us, as we had been saving dimes. As I look back now, we were two crazy kids! But we obeyed Jesus. I asked the Methodist Conference for a church and they said yes. I applied to Temple Seminary and was accepted.

We were married on February 25, 1956.in Erie. Thanks to May Olsen, a friend of Sandy's family, who loaned us her apartment with a stocked refrigerator, and her car for our weekend honeymoon. Meanwhile my folks were driving to Erie in the snow, and got a ticket in Meadville, PA from some crazy cop. My mom was scared to death on the icy roads and said "if I didn't have the ring with me, we'd turn around and go home." Dave Naglee was my best man and Sandy's brother, John, and my brother-in-law, Evan, were ushers. Audrey McLaughlin was our maid of honor and my sister, Peggy and Sandy's friend, Pat Lundfelt were bridesmaids. Our wedding reception was fancy sandwiches, cookies, punch and wedding cake – a far cry from weddings today. With all the money they spend today many are not as happy as we were and are. We are about to celebrate our 62nd anniversary in 2018. The next day was Sunday and my wife wanted to go to a church about 45 miles away, served by Rev. John Olexa. He had been the pastor at summer camp in Findley Lake, NY when she accepted Christ. It was a small church in Cochranton, PA. When Johnny saw us in the congregation he asked us to give our testimony, so we did. When we returned the car back to May they asked us how we liked the stones in the hubcaps. We were so much in love we heard nothing! We were two happy and blessed kids.

I mentioned my sister, Peggy and husband as being in our wedding. Peggy and Evan were married three months before e were and Peggy's husband, Evan Crook, and I always had a good time talking mostly about our Lord Jesus and sports. Later we were to have our first three children only a couple months apart which meant they grew up being good friends.

The next step was to get us and our wedding presents to New Jersey. We called Mayflower and they packed three large barrels of gifts, and shipped them to Collingswood. We took a Greyhound Bus from Erie to Collingswood. Sandy took a Dramamine as she suffered from motion sickness, then slept most of the way. I thought I had married a girl with sleeping sickness, but she did wake up when we arrived and is the greatest wife I could have ever had.

We rented an apartment in Westmont and that was a real fiasco! We could not empty the bathtub with water after 9:00 o'clock as the landlady said it kept her awake. Her rosebushes all died because "we" planted a couple tomato plants in "the assigned spot." Sandy got a job as secretary to the President of Tartan Foods in Camden for $50 per week and I continued working at the mission, with a raise from $10 to $25 a week. So, we were in the chips! That summer brought many new experiences – we bought our first car (and paid cash), were expecting our first child and as I had been in touch with the District Superintendent to get a church, Dr. Buck called and said I would be assigned as Pastor of the Fourth Methodist Church in Millville, NJ, and a smaller church in Center Grove.

Chapter V

I would like to tell you about the churches we served. Each one was different, and the Lord blessed at each appointment. Fourth Church was a small church, the only one in South Millville. This church was very important because I was young and inexperienced at being a pastor. I travelled with three or four other young pastors to seminary in Philadelphia three or four days per week while I was serving as pastor of these two churches. I preached three times a week at Fourth Church and at 3:00 PM Sunday afternoon at Center Grove. During the eight years we lived in Millville three of our four children were born: David, Stephen and Susan. The people of the church loved and accepted them. Sandy took the children to all of these services until Susan was born. Three o'clock Sunday afternoon became too much. The big blessing at Fourth Church was John Mulford and his family. They loved us and took us right in. John was 72 years old, but still very active. I knew John supported my preaching of the Gospel. That made a real difference If John had not supported us it would have been very difficult. Praise God for families such as this who support their pastor.

The first time I gave an altar call for people to receive Jesus as their Savior, six young people came to the altar. As I was praying with them, I looked up and there were six more praying at the altar. I prayed with them also and my heart was truly aflame. This was why I was in the ministry! Later I found out that the second six had left the church and were outside talking. John had asked them if they knew Christ as their Savior and they said "no." So John said "you better get back in there." That was such a blessing to me!

The parsonage was not new, but was lean and in very good condition. We were right next to the Armstrong Glass Factory which ran twenty-four seven. They were closed on Christmas Eve and day. That night we had trouble sleeping because it was so quiet. The parsonage had a washing machine, but no dryer. Sandy's hands became all cracked and sore from hanging diapers and other wash out in the cold, so one day we took a trip up to Sears in Vineland and purchased a dryer on time. So many good things I could say about Fourth Church and Millville. We were very happy there for almost eight years and although there were other churches we could have moved to during this time, we stayed. Everyone was very happy when we were able to build a new Sunday School wing and it was paid for in three years.. I spent many nights with the youth of the church as Sandy stayed home with our three, but she never complained. The Lord was gracious and many souls were saved. and some family's saved.

Millville already had a city-wide Vacation Bible School which was held in ten different locations throughout the city. We all used Scripture Press VBS materials. My job as director included getting all the teaching materials from Kites Christian Bookstore in Camden. That meant two or three flying trips to Camden each of the two weeks. Also I needed to visit each location, get their attendance figures, collect the daily offering which I turned over to the treasurer, and see what additional supplies they needed. All of this had to be done by 11:30 AM in order to get an article written and delivered to the local paper where it would be delivered yet that day. It was a lot of work, but we were getting God's Word to about 1400 children each day. While I was running the city-wide school, Sandy was directing the largest one in the city which was held at our church. We even used the classrooms on the first floor of Bacon School which was just across the street.

After three years I graduated from seminary and was ordained as a full-time elder in the United Methodist Church. This service was held on the music pier in Ocean City. We got to know a lot of other young couples starting out in the ministry as we were.

Chapter VI

Three and a half years later the District Superintendent offered to move us to East Camden to serve Bethel UM Church. We had no reason to move, but felt it was God's will at that time. It was nice to be near Collingswood and my family. Bethel was practically a new brick church and parsonage. The people received us graciously and we had a good ministry. As I look back at that time - 1964-69, I remember most of all our ministry with the youth. We had some really good spiritual adult advisors and 30 to 40 young people. We had good spiritual meetings and many fun times. About 35 of our youth went to our church camp at Malaga, NJ each summer, and there were some deep surrenders to Christ. During this time Jerry McFarland was saved and called to the ministry, and others were called to the ministry or mission field. I remember going caroling one Christmas Eve from midnight to two AM in the snow. I remember preaching to Senior-high's at Malaga. Sandy and I did about every job at Malaga during those many happy days. I even served on the Board of Directors and was president a couple years.

Tom and Ada Brown were deep Christians and very supportive of our ministry. Their two daughters, Beverly (who later married Jerry McFarland) and Barbara, donated many hours of baby-sitting while we attended church functions. We kept in touch with the Browns until the Lord took them home to be with the Lord.

The District Superintendent came around again in 1969 asking us to move to St. John's Church in Turnersville (now known as Washington Township). I told them I would rather not. Can you imagine wanting to stay in Camden instead of going to Turnersville? Well, I drove down to St. John's to meet the committee and things were quite a mess. No one on the committee had a key to the main building so we met in the sheet metal youth building. The previous pastor had been asked to leave after only a few months. I never understood why, but it made me wonder. We had a friendly meeting and they asked me to become their pastor. I told them I would pray about it and drove home. Later I met with all the District Superintendents and still told them I did not want to go. They were very fine and asked me to take an additional twenty-four hours to think about it again. On the way home, on Route 70, I passed the area where I knew Olive and Gus Gilbert had moved. I knew Gus would be at work, but I wanted to talk and pray with Olive. I was deeply impressed with her prayer life and deep walk with the Lord Jesus. I was still leaning toward staying in Camden. We talked and prayed and I drove on home to Camden and Sandy. As I drove along by myself, meditating on the Lord, slowly the assurance came "go." So when I got home I talked to Sandy about how I felt. She agreed, as always and I called the D.S. with a "yes, we will go." When we arrived there we began to find out what was really going on. The attendance was really low and there were two piles of unpaid bills. They had a mortgage due each month for the new building and they were having trouble making the payments. The real problem was that the spiritual life of the congregation was real low. There were many other things I could say, but no need here. I decided to do what I always did – preach the Gospel straight out of the Bible and meet the people in their homes. Most of the people, old and young, were blessed by the preaching. I did face some opposition from those who did not want to hear about accepting Jesus as their Savior to be saved. That was nothing new and soon resolved itself. New people would move into the community, come to church, visited by the pastor that week and they would continue to come and hear the preaching of God's Word. Many received Christ in a personal way and wanted to be involved in the church.

Our family was two boys and one girl as we left Camden and we were expecting a fourth. We wanted a girl to "even things up" but the Lord had other ideas and gave us another boy, Daniel.

St. John's Church was growing and many were showing real

spiritual growth, but we heard about a new United Methodist movement called "Lay Witness Mission" where the church would invite other U.M. Lay persons who had a real personal experience with Christ. They would come from near and far at their own expense. We were to supply housing and meals for the "witnesses". It opened on Friday evening with dinner and some personal testimonies. Then there were small group meetings in the homes of our people on Saturday morning. Saturday night there were more small groups. Each time our visiting witnesses would tell how Jesus had personally changed their lives and their families. Well, it was a deep moving of God in our church. On Sunday morning the leader of the team would preach a sermon. When he gave an invitation to come to the altar and receive Jesus Christ there was a great response. I remember very clearly the altar was full of seekers, about four deep and about half way up each aisle there were people on their knees crying out to God. Our church came on fire for God.

My wife and some of the girls began a small group Bible Study in a home once a week. The group grew and split into two groups. More and more girls came and more groups sprung up. Some came from our church, other churches, and even many Catholics. We never told them to leave their church, but to go to whatever church they wanted. Some came to our church and stirred the flame. Some went to the Catholic Church and spread the flame there. There were so many Catholic girls involved that when they dedicated their new church, I was asked to preach one night.

We had about eighteen women's groups, the men's 6:00 A.M. breakfast group on Wednesday and several small groups of youth. We were seeking a spiritual youth pastor to minister to our youth. We were greatly blessed when we were able to get Mark Fieger. Mark had just graduated from Asbury Seminary, and "Mark, the shark" was a great blessing to all the youth and to all the church.

Since the previous pastors had not been giving much attention to receiving new members into the church we assumed there should be a class on church membership. Always we emphasized that to join the church you must receive Christ as Savior and live your life as His disciple. After several classes, one Sunday we received sixty people into the membership of the church with their commitment to serve Jesus. The people were confounded! They had never seen that many people join on one Sunday.

The church continued to grow spiritually and numerically. All the bills were paid. A large Adult Sunday School included the parents of many of our youth.

We had a seminar on the Holy Spirit for pastors. This was led by Ross Whitesell, from the National Board of Discipleship as the speaker. About fifteen pastors came and only God knows the impact on their churches.

The church continued to grow. More and more people joined the church, but not sixty at a time. We had regular altar calls to be saved and more and more people responded. On our staff, besides the pastor and youth pastor we also had a secretary, janitor, business manager, and Christian counsellor. We also had a nursery school and staff with about fifty children. There were so many special things happening I cannot include them all.

One event I cannot overlook. Joe Coffini was a pharmacist and manager of the local drugstore. I had joined Rotary with the desire to share Christ with men in the business world. I had been attending for several years without much opportunity to share Christ. One morning I spoke to Sandy from the shower, saying "I'm going to quit Rotary today. I had joined to be a witness and it's not working." That noon time at the regular Thursday Rotary meeting Joe came to my table and said, "Howard, I've got to talk to you. I'm so depressed." We went to my car after the meeting and after talking and answering his questions, Joe asked Jesus to come into his heart. His wife, Betty, was already a Christian and had been praying for Joe. What a thrill to me to see Joe and his wife happy in the Lord. This was only one person out of many. Praise God, Jesus gets all the glory!

Duffield's Farm Marked is located in Washington Township, but we had never been to the market and did not know them. One Sunday someone pointed them out to me as being the Duffield's. I met them and they said immediately "we are going to continue to worship God in this church". They proceeded to be a great help to the church and personal friends. Wes Kandle owned a camp ground next to Duffield's farm. Soon, Wes, his wife, and family started to attend church and soon St. John's was their church also. There were two other large farms in the township, the Kuhn's and the Smith's, who also became part of the church. Because Washington Township was a transient community we were always having new people come to the church and occasionally moving to other areas.

During the thirteen years we pastored St. John's our four children were active in sports at all levels and we went to the games as often as we could. That also gave us an opening in the township. These were busy years as the church was able to build a new educational wing and a new parsonage as we added more staff. On a more personal note, each year the Rotary Club elected a "Man of the Year", and in 1981 I was extended that honor. I had no thought that this would happen, but to me it showed that this church was involved in the community and people wanted to worship here or were receptive to the church.

Chapter VII

After nine wonderful years at St. John's the District Superintendent asked me if we would be interested in serving St. Paul's Church in Brick, NJ. I did not even know where it was! Sandy and I drove up to Brick, about seventy five miles, and met with the PPR committee. They had had some problems with their current pastor and were glad for us to come, but I did not feel led to go. I had always served in South Jersey churches and the general idea around here was that the churches further north were spiritually cold. After praying about our decision I told the DS I would rather stay at St. John's and they said fine. Three years later they again asked me about moving to St. Paul's. They did not even remember having asked me previously. Sandy and I had no reason to leave St. John's but we were rather open to moving as we felt thirteen years was long enough. You stay too long and it is hard for the next minister. So we went up to Brick again. Again they wanted us to come and we agreed it was God's will for us. Our son, Dave, was living in VA.. Steve was not living at home at this time, and Sue and Dan were home. It made it hard for them, but we had to follow God's leading.

St. Paul's was a big change from St. John's! The last service at St. John's was a real out-pouring of God's Spirit. People were seeking God at the altar. The choir sang a special song for Sandy and another one for me. There was much love and many tears. The first Sunday at St. Paul's was very different. I think they thought I was a "hick" being from South Jersey, so I said from the pulpit, "see, I have shoes on." Then as I preached they were very staid and I was used to people being moved and saying "Amen." Suddenly I stopped in in the middle of the sermon and said "Do you folks say amen?" One lady said "We will" and they did. Although things started rather cold up there, they soon warmed up. Milton and Barbara Estelle were leaders. I could always talk to Milt when I wanted to know how things were going and Barb was the director of the choir. She always did a great job with the music and Milt told me later that Barb accepted Christ as her Savior as we ministered there.

One thing about St. Paul's - I really liked the sanctuary as a place to worship. The main altar was quite long and wide. Directly over the altar there hung a large wooden cross. There was a kneeling pad all around the table and we could get about 30 people kneeling at the altar for communion at one time. By this time I was wearing a white robe and red stole and still preaching the same old Gospel of Jesus Christ and His saving blood. It was a good place to worship the Living God.

One big factor was the Christian School. They previously had a pre-school but the people and I wanted a real Christian School, grades one to six. We discussed it and all the ramifications. We brought it to the Charge Conference for approval. The District Superintendent said "Methodist Churches don't have Christian Schools". I knew this wasn't true. One woman tried to defeat it by saying some untrue things at the meeting, even attacking me. She was just opposed to the whole idea. Well, I knew I had the votes because the people wanted it. The vote carried and we had our Christian School. Donna Kozlowski was the headmaster and Faye Schmidle was her secretary. Most of the teachers were active in our church. The school grew rapidly and had a good reputation among the people of all churches, even Roman Catholic. Each time they signed up children for the next year, the line formed about 4:00 AM. The school is still growing and teaching children God created them and Jesus died for them which the public school will not do. They now have grades one to eight and have built a gym and more classrooms.

We had had five Lay Witness Missions at St. John's and they were influential in lifting the whole spiritual life of the churches. I waited a few years and we had our first LWM at St. Paul's. It was ef fective, and we had two more, resulting in spiritual growth of the whole church.

During the last couple years in Brick I was burdened by the fact that we were reaching women, but not as many men. The Lord laid it on my heart to pick out about three to five men at a time who showed some spiritual life. We met each Tuesday evening from about 7:00 to 9:30. I aimed to pour into them everything the Lord had taught me. This included Scripture study, prayer, personal witnessing, family life and applying Biblical truths to current events and family Bible reading. The men gobbled it up! One guy worked in NYC. He took a bus out of Brick at 7:00 AM, got back to Brick at 7:00 PM and came directly to the meeting at church without supper. I usually took him home in my car because he lived in the next town. I guess I did this with about three or four groups. Every one of these men took spiritual leadership in the church. One especially was Bob Hagar. At the end of one of our classes he came to me and said "I want to do something." (I saw he was thinking of riding his bike to CA for some charity). He caught me flat-footed. I went home and told Sandy. She reminded me that Jack Hamilton was getting ready to take a mission team to Haiti and we decided to pursue that idea. I suggested it to Bob and he was ready to go immediately. So Sandy, Bob and I joined Jack's team of about 18 people including a medical doctor and several nurses. This was about 1985 and we had a glorious time, never to be the same.

What caused this? Getting into deep scriptural teaching which gives a person a caring heart for the world. Bob Hagar was really grasped with a missionary heart. His regular business was steel erection and his company had several cranes. He told me he no longer wanted to make money from his business, in fact he was willing to give all his time and resources to missions. But he did say he would keep the business for his two boys, which he did, and they still run it. Bob made several mission trips to Haiti and took several others from our church with him. They, too, became fired up for Haiti and more involvement. Bob was so moved to share Jesus in Haiti, he formed his own mission board and began plans for a mall medical clinic in

Port-a-Prince, Haiti. Then, beyond our human understanding, Bob got cancer and soon went to be with the Lord. Our hearts were broken for Bob and Sue Hagar. This whole Haiti vision was nothing unusual – it was the result of many fathers becoming New Testament Christians. It sets your heart on fire for the lost world Jesus died for and your whole life changes. After Bob died his board continued his dream in Haiti and also some home mission work there in Brick.

Sandy and I were deeply encouraged in the Gospel by Bill & Judy Propert, Terry and Nancy Penrod, Ralph and Ruth Baker, Stan and Donna Kozlowski, Suzanne Smoot, Norris and Ruth Blair and many others. We had gone to St. Paul's with many concerns, especially the spiritual atmosphere in the northern part of the state in the Methodist Church. We found again that Jesus is the same today as always and the Gospel works anywhere if you just cut loose and let it go.

Chapter VIII

At that time you could retire at age 62 or 65.We had planned to retire at age 65, which would have given us 13 years at St. Paul's, the same at St. John's. Brother Paul vanderLoo had retired five years before and had served the Union Chapel by the Sea at 55th and Asbury in Ocean City. This was an all year round, part time position. He had a good experience there and now wanted to retire completely. We were very surprised when he asked us to follow him as pastor at the Union Chapel. At first we hesitated because we really wanted to retire at 65. We prayed much about this. Things were falling into place - our new home outside of Bridgeton in Upper Deerfield was finished and we saw that things could work out to leave St. Paul's. The people in Ocean City wanted us to come and so we felt God leading us to retire from the United Methodist Church at age 64 and move to Bridgeton. It was one hour from Bridgeton to Ocean City. We drove down Sunday morning for worship and some visiting in the afternoon. We drove down Wednesday morning for Bible Study, some visiting and other concerns. We went back home Wednesday or Thursday. When we stayed overnight we stayed at my sister and husband's home in the summer and next door at John and Betsy Sandberg's home in the winter.

The people at the Chapel received the Gospel in a fine way and we had a good ministry for six years with them. We became especially close with a group of young adults who wanted a Bible Study for their age group. We met on Tuesday evening at several different homes and this was a real blessing to see their reaction to the Gospel. Mike and Kathy Gallagher were the prime movers in this group. For a small, part-time church we were pleased with an attendance of about 100 in the winter and up to 300 in the summer.

In1 999 we were thinking it might be time to stop serving the church in Ocean City. We submitted our plans for retirement in April of 1999 and in May I had a heart attack. I was able to return to the pulpit for most of the summer, ending serving this church as pastor in October. At this point we lived in our home full-time. We really loved our home there as it was our first home as owners. Our boys built us a fine shed with which to keep our lawnmower and other tools. We are indebted to Trav Cossaboon who oversaw the building of our modular home. We regret the recent passing of our friend, Trav. We attended the Wesleyan Church there in Upper Deerfield. The pastor and wife, Dwight and Jane Mikesell were spiritually alive and personal friends. We met some dear Christian people there and enjoyed the church there from 1999 to 2001.

Chapter IX

Somewhere along the line we heard about the Wiley Christian Retirement Community in Marlton. We hated to think of leaving our first and only owned home in Upper Deerfield, but realized that as we grew older we might need medical care. We visited Wiley and talked over the financial arrangements. All the time we prayed about this big decision. We figured if we sold our home in Upper Deerfield for what it was worth, we could swing the deal at Wiley. Our real estate agent felt we were asking too much for that home. In fact, he said the people in his office laughed when he told them what we were asking. We were determined to sell the house at our figure or we would keep it and continue to live there. Again we prayed. In a few weeks we had a signed contract for our price. Praise God! We were packing up to move to Wiley on 9/11 when someone told us over the phone about the terrorist attacks in NYC, Washington and Pennsylvania

We moved into our Wiley Home at 24 Balsam Way October 2, 2001. Sandy got a job as a receptionist in the evenings which she did for 10 years and which she really enjoyed. She was and is still able to do things on the computer to help in the ministry here. We were amazed to have three bedrooms, three bathrooms, living room, dining room, loft and garage. We decided upon this house as we would be able to have children and grandchildren visit us overnight or come for family dinners. We met our fine neighbors and were very happy. As time went by, the grandchildren went away to college, got married etc. and families came to visit less often. In 2012 we realized we did not need such a big house and moved to a smaller, one floor house with no garage. It also helped with finances as Sandy was now leaving her job at Wiley. We now have two bedrooms - one for sleeping and one used for a den in which we have Sandy's computer and my desk and books. Wiley has many advantages. If anything breaks, we send in a work order and it gets fixed. In summer the grass is always cut and in winter the snow is quickly shoveled.

I got involved in a small Bible-teaching ministry called "Alpha" at the church that touched many lives for years. Wiley is a real nice place in which to live. We have met many new friends. About two years after we arrived, my sister, Peggy, and her husband, Evan, moved here also. This gave us a chance to be with them more often than we were able to do before. Evan has had health issues and after four years of suffering from an incurable infection, went to be with Jesus May 11, 2017.

We worship God at the Wiley Church with folks from Wiley and also all ages from the surrounding Marlton area. In 2005 a new large Health Care Building was built which included a large physical fitness area where we work-out to keep in shape. We both have back problems and Sandy had back surgery in 2011 and again in 2017. I have had several trips to the hospital, but we are both basically in good health from day to day. We say we are in good shape for the shape we're in!

Chapter X

It has not all been work. We camped for twenty years with our children. A friend, Jim Townsend, took us to Bermuda two times through his work. We were then able to be connected with Willowbank in Bermuda. and I served there four times as "Prophet of the Week" which gave us free accommodations. One time we took another group of forty from our church which was a free ride for us. We have also taken a train trip across Canada, and a trip to the Maritime Provinces. We went to Germany where Sandy's fourth through eleventh great grandparents lived, and to the church which they attended. We also had a trip to England, Scotland, Wales and Ireland. There we were able to visit the church in Dungannon where my grandmother, Margaret Reed, came from in 1888. We took trips with America's Keswick to FL, which included Billy Graham's Library in NC, and to Branson, MO. .

Our four children, David, Stephen, Susan and Daniel are all active in their local churches. David is an electrician by trade. He built his own house in Farnham VA and another in Lynchburg. He got his BA at age fifty-five, followed by a Masters at Lynchburg University, and now at sixty is working on his Doctorate. David and Barbara's children are Solomon, Samuel, Josiah and Joanna. Solomon and Danielle have Lydia, Melody, Isaac and Joseph. Solomon works at Contegix, LLC as DevOps Engineer. Sam and Leanne have Samuel, Jadon and Micah. Josiah and Sarah have Luke, Levi and Philip. Both Sam and Josiah are policemen in Lynchburg, VA where they live, and Joanna is a nurse. Steve graduated from Asbury University and Asbury Seminary and was ordained in the United Methodist Church. He has been teaching Bible in a large Christian School in Lexington, KY, where his wife, Kathy, also teaches fifth grade. Steve also pastors a small UM Church outside Lexington. Steve and Kathy had three children, Pete, Tommy and Maria. We were all broken hearted when they lost their oldest son, Pete in 2015. We commit him to the Lord. Pete had one son, Domenick, who Steve and Kathy are able to see on a regular basis. Tommy is an intern with Urban Hope in Philadelphia nd graduating from Grace College in May. Maria is a nurse and has just married Logan Shaftner. Susan graduated from Messiah College and now works in a Christian School in Lititz, PA while her husband, Jim, is an agent for State Farm. Sue and Jim have Jimmy, Rachel and David. Jimmy is married to Kristin and works for Mudd Love in Winona Lake, IN. Rachel is working for Grace College and is married to Charlie Miller who will finish seminary at Grace this May. Dan also graduated from Messiah Collee and works for an investment company, Morgan Stanley. He is an elder at The Church of the Savior and with his wife, Courtney, are leaders in "Alpha". Dan and Courtney have Joshua, Hannah and Abigail. From the four children thirteen grandchildren and eleven great grandchildren: I'm sure there will be others. Each one is precious and we love them all. It's hard to be so far away that we don't see some them very often. Each of our four children are different. We did not expect them to follow any set pattern we set. They all love Jesus and are raising their children to love Him too. They have been very good to us and we are so richly blessed to have such godly children.

Most of God's saints have gone through what they call "the dark night of the soul". Job was a biblical example but there have been many others through the centuries. I am no saint, except a saint in Christ Jesus, but from the time I was "down" just before Asbury through all the tough times when I could not get the experience I was seeking, until I said "yes" to taking a church, going to seminary and marrying Sandy, I was really down. I would not pray in public. Twice I was called on to pray in Dr. Hall's Bible Class at Houghton. Nothing. Silence. "Mr. Gifford, "Will you lead in prayer?" Silence. I was so embarrassed and so down. I went to church at Houghton's Wesleyan Church, but during that time I never took communion. I felt that my heart was not right with God and you do not take communion like that. It was hard and it was embarrassing, but I was being honest with God and my own conscience. There was no sin that I knew of and I had given myself the best I knew how but there was no answer. This went on for about five years. I knew Jesus as my Savior, I knew I was called to preach, but I had to be honest to my own heart. Sandy and I dated and enjoyed being together and eventually I told her my story. She was kind enough to keep dating me and praying for me. How did I get out of it? I searched the Scriptures every day and made the amazing discovery "Abraham believed God and it was accounted unto him for righteousness." Thus if I believed God as my Savior, I was in a right relationship with God. Then I had that morning in 1956 when I read Revelation, chapter 1 and Jesus said in effect "get going or lose out." I began to move in God's direction and things worked out. I never had the big "whoopee" experience, but as I began to obey God and I went to my first church, I was richly blessed with God's assurance in prayer and preaching. Over the years I learned that God did not give me the "whoopee" experience to satisfy me, but He purified me in Jesus' blood and gave me a compassion to seek to lead each person I met to know Jesus Christ in a personal walk.

From time to time a person is honored in some way! I insert the following items, not out of pride, but to bring glory to God and to prove that people do observe the effects of our lives. In 1981 the Washington Township named me as "Man of the Year". In 1990 the United Methodist Foundation for Evangelism awarded me the Denman Evangelism Award. After we were at Wiley for several years Sandy and I were given the Volunteer of the Year Award for 2007.

So, to sum up my life, Jesus Christ changed my life, called me to preach and gave me a hunger for a closer walk with Him. Jesus said in John 7:37-39 "Out of your innermost being will flow floods of living water (Holy Spirit)." I have found some of this, but I hunger for more. "To God be the glory, great things He has done."

To those who may read this autobiography. GOD HAS A GOOD PLAN FOR YOUR LIFE. Secure His forgiveness of your sin by accepting Jesus as your personal Savior. Also make a complete surrender of your life to follow His Plan. The Bible says that "all have sinned and fallen shot of the Glory of God (Romans 3:23). Also Christians are called "to offer ones life as a living sacrifice. The Holy Spirit is God's power to do this. (Acts 1:4, 5) (Romans 12:1)

Made in the USA
Columbia, SC
24 May 2018